KU-150-099

DO ANIMALS NEED UMBRELLAS?

This edition is published by Armadillo, an imprint of Anness Publishing Ltd, 108 Great Russell Street, London WC1B 3NA; info@anness.com

www.annesspublishing.com; twitter: @Anness_Books

If you like the images in this book and would like to investigate using them for publishing, promotions or advertising, please visit our website www.practicalpictures.com for more information.

© Anness Publishing Ltd 2015

All rights reserved. No part of this publication may be reproduced, stored in a retrieval system, or transmitted in any way or by any means, electronic, mechanical, photocopying, recording or otherwise, without the prior written permission of the copyright holder.

A CIP catalogue record for this book is available from the British Library.

Publisher: Joanna Lorenz
Designed by Helen James

PUBLISHER'S NOTE
The author and publishers have made every effort to ensure that this book is safe for its intended use, and cannot accept any legal responsibility or liability for any harm or injury arising from misuse.

Manufacturer: Anness Publishing Ltd,
108 Great Russell Street, London WC1B 3NA, England
For Product Tracking go to: www.annesspublishing.com/tracking
Batch: 7188-23411-1127

LONDON BOROUGH OF HACKNEY LIBRARIES	
HK12001864	
Bertrams	16/02/2016
J590.2	£4.99
	31/12/2015

DO ANIMALS NEED UMBRELLAS?

And other questions and answers about life in the wild

WRITTEN BY STEVE PARKER • ILLUSTRATED BY GRAHAM ROSEWARNE

ARMADILLO

Introduction

Do animals carry umbrellas or wear winter clothes?
Of course they don't! In nature, animals have to survive using
only their own bodies. This means that for an animal
to keep alive and healthy, its body must be fitted to the
conditions and places where it lives. We say that an animal is
adapted to its natural habitat. Creatures in cold climates have
thick fur, feathers or fat to keep them warm. Those in dry
places need to drink very little water. Animals in wet places
have waterproof fur, feathers, scales or skin to keep them dry.

Adaptation helps animals to survive. But it also limits the
places where they can live. Imagine a penguin in a desert!
It would be far too hot and would have no sea to swim in or
fish to eat. And a zebra would soon die from cold and hunger
if it was left on an Antarctic iceberg with no grass to eat.

Contents

Do animals...

DO ANIMALS...
Live in the woods?

Yes, they do. In fact, more creatures live in woods and forests, than anywhere else on Earth. Each type of natural place, such as a wood, a swamp, a grassland, a pond, a desert or an ocean, is called a habitat. Wood and forest habitats are the world's richest places for wildlife. The trees provide many kinds of foods, such as leaves, shoots, fruits and roots. They also give shelters, homes and nests to thousands of kinds of insects, birds, mammals and other animals.

The **hedgehog** could easily be called a 'woodhog'. This spiny, prickly relative of moles and shrews snuffles among the fallen leaves. It searches for slugs, snails, worms, grubs and other small snacks. The average hedgehog has about 5,000 sharp spines. It rolls up into a ball to protect itself from foxes and other predators.

Beware of the **brown bear**, especially a mother with her cub. To protect her offspring, she charges and fights anyone who comes near. Brown bears live in forests and mountain areas in northwest North America, where they are sometimes called grizzlies. They also live in parts of Europe and across northern Asia. Brown bears eat almost any food, from leaves and fruits, to insects, fish and young deer.

Deer, such as the **white-tailed deer**, are well adapted to life in open woodland, where they graze on shoots and leaves. When in danger, they can hide in the thick undergrowth, or race to safety among the tree trunks. As the deer runs from danger, the bright flash of white fur beneath its tail acts as a warning to other members of the herd.

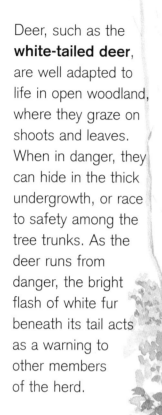

Have you heard a noise like a machine gun deep in the woods? It may be a **green woodpecker** 'drumming' on a tree, with a series of very fast pecks. The woodpecker makes tiny holes with its long, sharp beak. It searches under the bark for beetles, grubs and other small animals. Its skull and neck are very strong, so it does not get a headache!

The **grey wolf** was once common in woods across North America, Europe and Asia. However, many of these woods have been cut down for timber, firewood and farmland. People were also afraid of wolves, and wolves sometimes attacked farm animals. Many wolves were hunted and killed. Now they are rare in many places, especially Europe. They have been driven from forests, up into mountains and out into deserts.

7

DO ANIMALS...

Wear winter clothes?

In the winter, wild animals, unlike people, do not have the luxury of clothes. They survive the winter cold in any way they can. Many mammals change their natural fur coat in the autumn. The thinner hairs of the summer coat fall out and longer, thicker hairs grow in their place. The thick winter coat keeps the animal warm and dry, even in icy winds and heavy snow. Birds lose their coats too. They lose their summer feathers and grow thicker plumage for the winter.

The thickness of an animal's coat is important. So is its hue. **Ptarmigans** live in the far north, where the winter landscape is white with frost, snow and ice. So in winter the ptarmigan turns white. Its winter feathers help it to blend in with the background. This camouflage means the ptarmigan cannot be seen so easily. In summer, its brown plumage helps it to blend in among the grasses and twigs.

Siberia, in northern Asia, is one of the world's coldest places, even in summer. The **Siberian tiger** has the longest and thickest fur of any tiger. It is also the world's biggest tiger, more than 3.5m/11½ft from nose to tail-tip. In winter, its coat is very pale with thin stripes. This helps it to hide in the snow, as it creeps up on its prey. Siberian tigers now live only in a small area of north-east Asia, and they are very rare.

Hares are famous for their long ears. But the **snowshoe hare** of North America has quite short ears. Why? Because large body parts that stick out, such as ears and tails, lose a lot of heat. In cold places, animals need to keep in as much body heat as they can. This shows that body shape, as well as a thick, furry coat, is important.

The **musk ox** has very thick, very long fur to keep it warm. Each hair is longer than your arm. Musk oxen live in the far north of North America – from Alaska across to Greenland. The countryside is covered with ice and snow for most of the year. The oxen scrape away the snow with their hooves, to uncover plants to eat.

The **walrus** lives in the Arctic area around the North Pole. It swims in the icy seas and basks on frozen snow in the weak winter sun. But it has hardly any fur at all. So how does it stay warm? Under its skin, the walrus has a very thick layer of body fat, called blubber. This is very good at keeping in body heat. Whales also have thick blubber, for the same reason.

9

DO ANIMALS...
Need to drink water?

All animals need water to stay alive. No creature can survive without it. But not all animals need to drink water. Some can get the water they need from their food. This might be the watery saps and juices in plant food, or the blood and body fluids in animal food. Many desert animals get water in this way. They also lose very little water from their bodies, in their sweat, urine and droppings. However, when they find a pool, these animals drink as much as they can.

The **fennec fox** is the world's smallest fox. It is about the size of a pet cat and it lives in the Sahara and Arabian deserts. Like many desert animals, it saves as much of its body water as possible. It produces little urine, and its faeces, or droppings, are dry and hard. The huge ears listen for the tiny scrabblings of prey, such as mice and beetles. The fox's ears also help it to lose extra body heat.

The **camel** is well adapted for life in the desert. Its thick fur protects it from the heat and sunburn. Its wide feet stop it from sinking into the soft sand, and its long eyelashes keep windblown sand out of its eyes. When it finds water, at a well or in the pool of an oasis, a camel can drink 150 litres/ 264 pints in five minutes. That's almost twice the amount you have for your bath!

Ostriches are the biggest birds in the world. They live in the savannah grasslands and semi-desert areas of Africa. They feed on leaves, shoots, flowers and seeds, and get the fluid they need from their food. Ostriches can survive most conditions, as long as there are enough plants to eat.

The **thorny devil** lives in the desert regions of Australia. This lizard 'drinks' through its skin. During the cool night, dew forms on the ground and on the thorny devil's skin. Small grooves in its skin soak up water from the ground, and the network of fine grooves funnels this moisture to the lizard's mouth.

The Namib desert, in southwest Africa, is near the coast, where fog and mist blow in from the sea. The **Namib desert beetle** drinks by standing, head down, on a sand dune. Misty moisture droplets from the sea roll down its body into its mouth.

The **Arabian oryx** lives deep in the deserts of the Middle East. In the heat of the day, this small antelope finds shade under acacia trees. It scrapes the dry soil with its hooves to uncover food and moisture. In the night, when it's cooler, the oryx can walk up to 30km/18½ miles to find new feeding places.

Need air?

Not exactly. Animals need oxygen. This is an invisible gas. It's needed to make your body work. Oxygen helps to free the energy in the food that you have eaten and digested. All animals must have this energy to live, grow and move about. Oxygen makes up one-fifth of the air around us. Land animals get oxygen by breathing air into their lungs or similar body parts. Oxygen is also found in water. The fresh water of streams, ponds, rivers and lakes and the salt water of seas and oceans contain oxygen. Water animals can take in this oxygen through their gills or similar body parts.

The **seahorse** does not look like an ordinary fish. It has a horse-shaped head and a curly tail to grip seaweed or rocks. But like all fish, it has gills for breathing under the water. The gills are just behind the eyes. Water comes in through the mouth and flows over the gills. The gills take oxygen from the water into the body. The water flows out through gill slits on the sides of the head.

Dolphins live in water, but they cannot stay under for ever. This is because they are not fish, with gills. Dolphins are mammals, like us. They have warm blood, and lungs for breathing air, like us. Kept under water, they would drown, like us. A dolphin comes to the surface and breathes through its blowhole, on the top of its head.

Reptiles have lungs and breathe air just like birds and mammals. So reptiles that live in water need to come to the surface to take in fresh air. The **green turtle** is one of seven types of sea turtle. The others include the leatherback, hawksbill and loggerhead turtles. A green turtle can stay under the water for as long as an hour before it needs another breath of air.

Many other water creatures, besides fish, have gills for taking in oxygen from the water. An **octopus** has gills in the lower part of its 'head', which is really its whole body. The gills and other body parts are covered by a large, cloak-shaped flap of skin called the mantle.

Like all fish, the **great white shark** has gills on the sides of its head. The shark swims along with its mouth wide open. Water flows into its mouth, over the gills, and out through the row of gill slits on its 'neck'. Except, that is, when the shark bites, and its mouth is full of food. It must swallow the food quickly, or it will suffocate.

13

DO ANIMALS...
Live under the ground?

Yes, many do. Some live almost their entire lives under the ground. They rarely come up to the surface. They eat, rest, feed and breed in the dark world below your feet. Other animals make tunnels and burrows for their shelters and nests. They usually come out into the open air to find food and a mate. Some creatures make their homes deep in dark holes and caves. These underground homes are usually safe from the animal's enemies. The creatures living there are also protected from the worst of the weather.

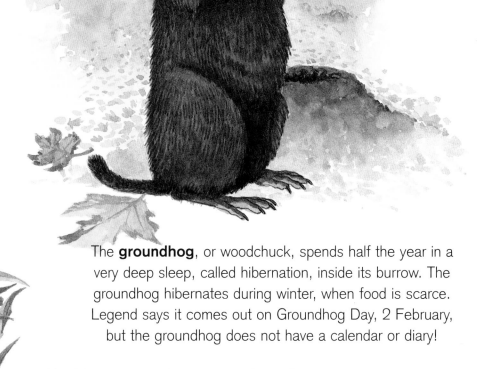

The **groundhog**, or woodchuck, spends half the year in a very deep sleep, called hibernation, inside its burrow. The groundhog hibernates during winter, when food is scarce. Legend says it comes out on Groundhog Day, 2 February, but the groundhog does not have a calendar or diary!

The **European mole** comes to the surface now and then, often after it has rained. It searches for worms and slugs among the damp plants. Most of the time, the mole looks after its tunnels, which may total 200m/656ft in length. It keeps the tunnels open, and eats the tiny creatures that live in the earth walls.

Many animals make burrows and holes. They usually have body parts that are adapted for digging. Can you guess how the **spadefoot toad** got its name? Each back foot has a flattened side, like a tiny shovel. The toad can dig itself straight down into loose soil and disappear in less than 20 seconds!

The **tuatara** is a type of reptile from New Zealand. It lives on a few rocky islands off the coast. This strange creature looks like a lizard, but it isn't. It belongs to a group of reptiles that were common millions of years ago, even before dinosaurs walked the Earth. Each tuatara lives in a burrow. It often shares its home with a petrel or other sea bird. The tuatara goes out at night to eat spiders and beetles, and the bird goes in for a night's rest!

Surely birds like to fly in the sky and perch in trees, rather than be dark and cramped? Not all birds. **Burrowing owls** live in dry grasslands. There are no trees for perching. So these small owls shelter and raise their chicks in a burrow. But they don't dig the burrow. They use an empty one, or they borrow or steal a ready-made burrow from another animal.

15

DO ANIMALS...
Fear heights?

Some people are afraid of high places such as cliffs, treetops and skyscrapers. If they see the ground far below, they get dizzy and feel ill and frightened. Yet many animals live on cliffs and mountains, and in treetops. It is their natural home. They never seem to become giddy or frightened. Which is just as well, otherwise they would soon fall and be injured or killed. An advantage of living in high places is that there are fewer predators trying to eat you. But there's often less food, too.

Bighorn goats run about on steep slopes near sharp drops. They leap around even when the rocks are slippery with rain or ice. Mountain goats have strong legs, and their large hooves grip the rocks well. These wild goats live in the mountains and snowy areas of North America. As soon as they are born, the baby goats learn to move safely over the rocks and boulders.

The **pika** looks like a guinea pig, but it really belongs to the same mammal group as rabbits and hares. Pikas live in mountains and rocky areas in Asia and western North America. In autumn, they scamper fearlessly about their mountain home, gathering plant food to store for winter.

16

The **condors** from North and South America are among the world's largest birds. Their wings measure 3m/ 10ft from tip to tip. A condor can soar for hours over the high peaks of the Andes and Rocky Mountains. The birds swoop down the valleys, looking for dead and dying animals to eat. When they get tired, which is very rare, they perch on the steepest rocky outcrop to rest.

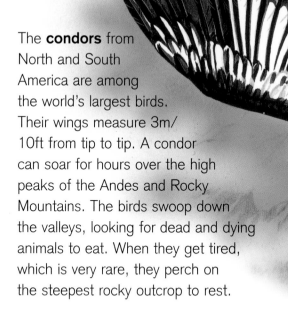

Llamas are very sure-footed animals. They can climb the steepest mountain paths. In South America, people use llamas in the same way that people in other places use sheep, cows and horses. Llamas are raised to give milk and wool, and for meat, fur skins and leather. Their droppings are even burnt as fuel. Llamas are also excellent pack animals. They carry heavy loads between villages along the steep tracks of the Andes, where road vehicles cannot go.

17

Wear spots and stripes?

Yes. And many animals have spotted or striped coats. These patterns help the animals to blend in with their background. We say that they are camouflaged. Such camouflage helps an animal to hide and survive. A predator that cannot easily be seen can creep up on its prey unnoticed. The camouflaged prey can hide from the hunter! Which one wins depends on which animal is quietest or most stealthy. Or, if it comes to a chase, which one can run the fastest.

The **pampas cat** lives in the grasslands, scrubs and forests of South America. This medium-size cat creeps through the dark night, eating any small animals it can catch. It feeds on insects, mice, rats and other small mammals, birds, lizards and their eggs. The cat's dark spots help to disguise its body shape in the shadows of the moonlit undergrowth. A pet tabby cat is blotched and striped for the same reason.

Few animals are as striped as a **zebra**! This close relation of the horse has dark brown stripes on a white background – or is it the other way round? The zebra blends in with the tall grasses and their shadows on the savannahs of Africa. Zebras live in groups or herds. When they spot danger, they panic and run. A predator, such as a lion, has great trouble picking out one victim from the flashing, dazzling mass of moving stripes!

18

Some animals have glaring spots or stripes. These are not for camouflage, but to show off and be seen clearly. The **ladybird or ladybug** is one. Its bright patterns are there to warn other animals that it tastes horrible. Birds and other animals soon learn this, and they leave them alone.

Hyenas have stripes and spots, but not on the same animal. The **striped hyena** (shown here) lives in northern Africa, the Middle East and India. The spotted hyena has spots instead of stripes. It lives in the grasslands of east and southern Africa. Both types of hyena are fierce hunters and scavengers. Their patterns are mainly for camouflage. They help the hyenas blend in among the dry grasses.

Some creatures are so huge and strong, that they do not need disguise or camouflage. The world's second biggest land animal is the very plain-skinned **rhinoceros**. Its large size, heavy weight, very thick skin and sharp nose horn serve to protect it. Hardly any predators dare to attack it. If they do, they get speared by its horn and trampled under its massive body.

19

Need umbrellas?

Have you been caught out in a rainstorm, without a coat or umbrella? You soon get wet and you feel cold and uncomfortable. This is because you are used to being dry, and your body is suited to dry places. Some animals are used to living in water. Their bodies are adapted to the wet. These animals can come out on land, but if they get too dry they soon feel uncomfortable. They are expert swimmers and they catch their food in the water. Some creatures, such as fish, must stay in water all the time. If they come out into the air, they cannot breathe. Within a few minutes they suffocate and die.

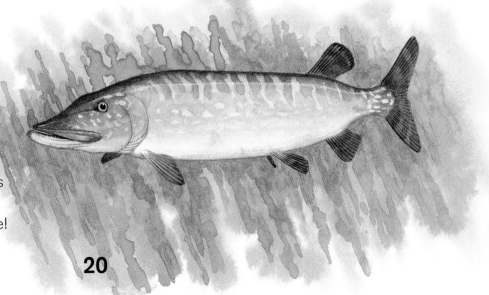

Swans are beautiful white birds that float on rivers and lakes. They swim using their webbed feet. Their feathers have a natural oily coating that keeps out water, so the swan stays dry. This bird often combs, or preens, its feathers with its beak. This helps to remove dirt and spread the oil over the swan's feathers.

The **pike** lives in waterweeds. Like all fish, the pike must always stay wet, but its body is protected from the water by a layer of hard scales and waterproof skin. Its gills, on the sides of its head, can only take in oxygen from the water. In air, the gills dry out and the pike dies. As a small fish swims past, the pike flicks its powerful tail, darts out, and opens its huge, sharp-toothed mouth. SNAP, the fish has gone!

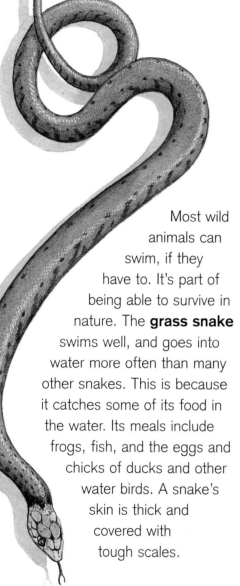

Most wild animals can swim, if they have to. It's part of being able to survive in nature. The **grass snake** swims well, and goes into water more often than many other snakes. This is because it catches some of its food in the water. Its meals include frogs, fish, and the eggs and chicks of ducks and other water birds. A snake's skin is thick and covered with tough scales.

The **water vole** is about the same size as a rat. It lives by the water, eating water plants and sometimes catching frogs and fish. It is a true vole, with a blunt nose, flat face and small, furry ears. The vole's thick, dark brown fur keeps it warm. The fur also contains natural oils and waxes, making its coat glossy and waterproof. The vole grooms its coat with its paws and teeth. This helps to keep the coat clean and to spread the oils over the fur.

Is that a harmless log in the water? No, it's an **alligator**. It is ready to grab any prey in its wide mouth. After it has fed, the alligator may crawl out on to a dry bank to sunbathe. It can live in wet or dry places, as its scaly skin helps protect it from getting wet or drying out.

21

Hang around in trees?

Forests cover large parts of the world. Huge numbers of animals live in these trees, especially in tropical rain forests. They range from tiny beetles, butterflies and tree frogs, to large snakes, birds and monkeys. Some of these creatures rarely come down to the ground. The trees provide all their needs – food of all kinds and drink in the form of rainwater pools trapped in branch forks. Leaves or tree holes provide shelter and there are many places to rest, nest and raise a family.

If you live among leaves, green skin is good for camouflage. The **green tree python** lies coiled firmly around a branch. It can stay very still for a long, long time. Other creatures forget it's there. If a bird, tree frog or other animal comes too near, the python quickly grabs its next meal.

The **orang-utan** seems to have four arms. It can grip and climb as well with its feet and legs as with its arms. This great ape lives in tropical rain forests on the islands of Borneo and Sumatra in South-east Asia. The orang-utan, often called the 'old man of the forest', moves slowly and carefully among the branches. It searches for wild fruits, such as figs, lychees and mangoes.

22

Crawl around as slowly as you can, and you still would not be as slow as a **sloth**. This creature is not lazy, it's just living life at its own speed. Its body is designed for hanging around in the trees of Central and South America. Its claws, like curved hooks, grip the branch tightly. Its fur slants the other way from the fur of most mammals, so that rain drips off easily. Sloths eat mainly leaves – slowly, of course.

It can be difficult to find a mate among the crowded leaves and twigs of the rain forest. So the male **blue bird of paradise** finds a small clearing among the branches. Here, he puts on an amazing dancing display. He hangs upside down, shakes his brilliant feathers and sings loudly. Females soon gather, and the male chooses a mate.

If you constantly climb through trees, four limbs may not always be quite enough. So the **tamandua** (tree anteater) has five. The fifth is its tail. The tail is thick, long, muscular and strong. It is also prehensile, which means it can wrap around and grip objects such as tree branches. Like its ground-living cousins, this anteater feeds on termites and ants. It searches them out both in trees and on the ground.

23

DO ANIMALS...
Play in the waves?

Do you enjoy the seaside? You can paddle and splash, and have fun in the sun. But would you like to live there, even in winter? We are not really adapted to seashore life. But many animals thrive on the coast. They do not mind the hot sun or the cold wind and rain. They can survive being covered by salt water as the tide comes in. They can also survive being dry as the tide goes out. Such animals live on the seashore all the time. They are adapted to life in this ever-changing habitat. Other animals just come to the shore to rest or feed.

Limpets

Mussels

Whelk

Many creatures that live in rock pools have hard shells to protect their soft bodies. They are called molluscs. **Limpets** cling so strongly to the rock that not even a huge wave can knock them off. **Mussels** are fixed to the rock by stringy threads, and they filter the sea water for food. The **whelk**, a type of sea snail, then eats the mussels!

Common seals feed in the ocean, chasing fish and other sea creatures. When the sun comes out, they swim to the beach. They wriggle and heave themselves out of the water, to sunbathe on the sand. But they keep a sharp watch for trouble, especially at breeding time. A seal pup can swim well just a few minutes after it is born. Like other baby mammals, it feeds on its mother's milk. It can drink this on land, or in the water.

24

Many birds live along seashores. They have long legs to wade through the waves and shallows, and long beaks to probe for food in the sand and mud. **Oystercatchers** feed on oysters, and also on mussels, clams and similar shellfish. They peck hard at the shells to make a hole, then eat the soft flesh inside.

Shore fish, such as the **rock goby**, are very tough. They have to cope with crashing waves, rolling stones, moving sand and being stranded as the tide goes out. The goby has thick, slippery skin and strong, spiny fins. It can skip and slither across the slimy rocks, out of the water, from one pool to another.

Recycling is a good idea, and **shore crabs** are nature's recyclers on the seashore. They are scavengers. They eat all kinds of plants and animals, whether sick, dying or dead. Then the crabs themselves become food for birds, fish and other sea creatures.

25

Get stuck in the mud?

Yes, but only when they want to. Many people dislike mud. They think it is dirty – it gets on to shoes, socks and clothes. But many animals love mud. It often contains worms, snails and other foods. A mud bath in the swamp is cooling on a hot day. Wallowing in mud also helps to get rid of fleas, lice and other pests on the skin. And it is easy to dig down into mud and hide there, if danger threatens. No wonder so many creatures are stick-in-the-muds!

Why are these fish out of water? They are **mudskippers**. They hop, skip and jump across the mud of tropical shores. Then they splash into a pool, and flip out again. Mudskippers can survive out of water for many minutes. They breathe using their gills, by carrying tiny pools of water in their cheek-like gill chambers. They eat small worms, shellfish and other creatures on and in the mud.

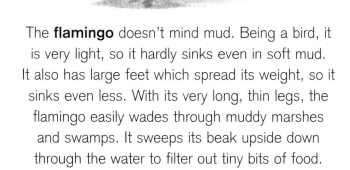

The **flamingo** doesn't mind mud. Being a bird, it is very light, so it hardly sinks even in soft mud. It also has large feet which spread its weight, so it sinks even less. With its very long, thin legs, the flamingo easily wades through muddy marshes and swamps. It sweeps its beak upside down through the water to filter out tiny bits of food.

26

Warthogs walk and wallow in waterholes in eastern and southern Africa. They splash and soak in the water, and rub themselves with mud. This helps them cool down and keeps off flies and pests. They also search for roots, seeds and small animals in the sticky, soft soil. Predators, such as lions, cannot race through the mud to hunt them, so the warthogs are fairly safe. But they must beware of mud-covered crocodiles!

Crab-eating macaques really do eat crabs, plus snails, slugs, shellfish and anything else they find in the muddy banks of rivers, lakes and coasts in South-east Asia, where they live. This monkey is also called the long-tailed macaque. It thrives on many other foods such as leaves, fruits, and small animals like insects, lizards and mice. It also eats farm crops, so it's not popular in some places.

Many turtles, such as the **yellow mud turtle**, are mud specialists. They walk slowly through the swamp, munching water plants. Sometimes they catch a frog, fish or other small creature. If danger threatens, the turtle quickly digs itself into the sticky mud, so only the hard, tough top of the shell shows. If a predator tries to pull it out, the turtle snaps back hard!

27

Bump into each other in the dark?

Not very often. We stumble about and bump into things in the dark. That's because our bodies are adapted to being active by daylight and asleep during darkness. Humans are diurnal. Some animals sleep by day and come out at night. They are nocturnal. They are adapted to finding their way in darkness without a stumble or a bump. Their huge eyes see in very dim light. Their large whiskers feel for objects. Their keen noses sniff food and their sensitive ears hear danger.

Little blue penguins are the smallest penguins, only 30cm/12in tall. They live in tunnels along the seashores of southern Australia. They do not finish fishing and feeding in the sea until after dark. Then they waddle quickly across the beach to the safety of their burrows in the dunes.

The **bushbaby** of African forests was named from its night-time cry. It sounds like the screaming wail of a human baby. This hand-sized relative of monkeys also looks babyish with its huge eyes, which help it to see in the dark, and snub nose. But a crying bushbaby is not in pain. It is warning other bushbabies to keep out of its own small area, or territory, of forest, where it lives and feeds.

The **nightjar** is well named. At night it sings its jarring, churring song – it sounds like a small motorcycle engine! At night, too, the nightjar swoops over fields and between trees as it catches its food of flying insects. Its good eyesight and wide beak help this nocturnal hunting. By day, the nightjar sits quite still on the ground or in a tree. It looks like a small pile of dead leaves or a stumpy branch.

Bats, such as the **horseshoe bat**, avoid bumps not by seeing, but by squeaking and listening. The bat makes very high squeaks, clicks and other sounds. The echoes of these sounds bounce off nearby objects, such as trees and walls or moths and mosquitoes. The bat listens to the pattern of these echoes. It can then find its way or can catch food, even in total darkness.

Most cats, such as this **black panther**, are adapted to hunt at night. They can see well in the dark. On a night with little moonlight, few creatures would see the black panther creeping silently towards them. This big cat is really a very dark type of leopard. Bright daylight reveals its black spots against the slightly paler fur. In parts of South-east Asia, nearly half of all leopards are black. In Africa, black leopards are much rarer.

Like living with people?

Some do, such as our cats, dogs and other pets. Also, some wild creatures seem to like people. They live in and around our houses, shops, factories and other buildings. They come into our gardens and parks. They share our food, sometimes whether we like it or not! These familiar animals may become so common that they are pests. We try to get rid of them, but they are very wary and difficult to catch. They keep well away from people. These creatures do not like us, but they do like the food, shelter and surroundings that humans provide.

Wherever there are people, there are rats and mice. The **black rat**, or ship rat, is very common in warmer areas. It comes out at night, and it can easily climb up walls and ropes. It gnaws its way into food stores and leaves its droppings and urine, which spoil the food. The black rat also carries pests, such as fleas, and spreads diseases.

The **grey squirrel** is a common sight in gardens, parks and woods, even in the middle of cities. It often comes to feed at bird tables. It looks cute and cuddly, but the grey squirrel has sharp teeth and claws, and it can bite and scratch hard. It damages trees and bushes by gnawing their bark.

The **Moorish gecko** is a type of lizard found in Mediterranean and Adriatic countries, and North Africa. It can climb well and clings to walls, windows and doors with its sucker-like toes. Several kinds of geckoes come into houses and walk across the walls and ceilings, especially at night. They cause no harm. They even help by eating flies.

Before there were houses, **house martins** made their mud nests on steep cliffs and rocky outcrops. But a house wall does just as well. The martin clings to the wall with its small, sharp claws. The house's overhanging roof protects the bird and its cup-shaped nest from the rain. House martins eat small insects, which they catch in flight. Martins also make loud twittering noises, especially early in the morning!

Around the world, people try to get rid of **cockroaches** by using poisons, sprays and traps. But these insects are great survivors and they are very difficult to kill. They get into houses, kitchens, food stores, factories and other warm buildings. They come out at night and feed on almost anything, even paper and leather.

31

Do people need umbrellas?

Yes – because we are not adapted to live in just one habitat, such as a rain forest. We can survive in more places than any other animal – from mountains and moorlands, to swamps and snowfields. However, we do not usually live as part of nature. We build houses and equip them with heating or air conditioning. When we go out in cold weather we put on warm clothes. When it is very hot we wear a sun hat – and, of course, when it rains we carry an umbrella!

Index